Knock Knock Jokes for Kids

*200+ FUNNIEST Knock
Knock Jokes for Kids*

SUPER FUNNY KNOCK KNOCK JOKES FOR KIDS

First edition. April 14, 2023.

Copyright © 2023 Issam Ramzi.

ISBN: 979-8215884508

Written by Issam Ramzi.

Introduction

Knock Knock Jokes for Kids: 200+ FUNNIEST Knock Knock Jokes for Kids is a book filled with humorous knock-knock jokes that are suitable for children. The book contains over 200 original jokes that will have kids laughing out loud and sharing with their friends and family. The jokes are organized in a way that is easy to read and understand, making it a great choice for kids who are just learning to read. This book is perfect for parents, teachers, and anyone who wants to bring a little bit of laughter and joy into the

lives of children. Whether it's for a long car ride, a family game night, or just a quick laugh, "Knock Knock Jokes for Kids" is sure to provide hours of fun and entertainment.

Knock, knock.

Who's there?

Boo.

Boo, who?

Don't cry, it's just a joke!
Knock, knock.

Who's there?

Alpaca.

Alpaca who?

Alpaca the suitcase, you load up the car!
Knock, knock.

Who's there?

Lettuce.

Lettuce who?

Lettuce in, it's cold out here!

Knock, knock.

Who's there?

Gorilla.

Gorilla who?

Gorilla me a hamburger, please!
Knock, knock.

Who's there?

Avenue.

Avenue who?

Avenue heard this one before?
Knock, knock.

Who's there?

Figs.

Figs who?

Figs the doorbell, it's broken!

Knock, knock.

Who's there?

Tank.

Tank who?

**You're welcome!
Knock, knock.**

Who's there?

Yukon.

Yukon who?

**Yukon say that again, I didn't hear you!
Knock, knock.**

Who's there?

Orange.

Orange who?

Orange you going to answer the door?

Knock, knock.

Who's there?

Nobel.

Nobel who?

No bell, that's why I knocked!
Knock, knock.

Who's there?

Cash.

Cash who?

No thanks, I prefer peanuts.
Knock, knock.

Who's there?

Honeybee.

Honeybee who?

Honeybee a dear and get me a soda?

Knock, knock.

Who's there?

Gouda.

Gouda who?

**Gouda you like to know!
Knock, knock.**

Who's there?

Lion.

Lion who?

**Lion in bed, not feeling well.
Knock, knock.**

Who's there?

Wanda.

Wanda who?

Wanda you think you're doing? Open the door!

Knock, knock.

Who's there?

Leaf.

Leaf who?

**Leaf me alone, I'm trying to take a nap.
Knock, knock.**

Who's there?

Lena.

Lena who?

**Lena little closer and I'll tell you another joke!
Knock, knock.**

Who's there?

Nana.

Nana who?

Nana your business who's there!

Knock, knock.

Who's there?

Harry.

Harry who?

**Harry up and open the door!
Knock, knock.**

Who's there?

Sherlock.

Sherlock who?

**Sherlock your door, I can't get in!
Knock, knock.**

Who's there?

Bo.

Bo who?

Bo-ris Johnson!

Knock, knock.

Who's there?

Owls.

Owls who?

Yes, they do!
Knock, knock.

Who's there?

Boomerang.

Boomerang who?

I'll come back to that joke later!
Knock, knock.

Who's there?

Frank.

Frank who?

Frank you for letting me in!

Knock, knock.

Who's there?

Cashew.

Cashew who?

**Bless you!
Knock, knock.**

Who's there?

Iva.

Iva who?

**Iva sore hand from knocking so long!
Knock, knock.**

Who's there?

Dewey.

Dewey who?

Dewey have to keep telling knock-knock jokes?

Knock, knock.

Who's there?

Ken.

Ken who?

Ken you open the door please?
Knock, knock.

Who's there?

Gorilla.

Gorilla who?

Gorilla me a sandwich, please?
Knock, knock.

Who's there?

Candice.

Candice who?

Candice door open or what?

Knock, knock.

Who's there?

Kanga.

Kanga who?

Kanga-roo, how are you?
Knock, knock.

Who's there?

Toad.

Toad who?

Toadally awesome!
Knock, knock.

Who's there?

Omelette.

Omelette who?

Omelette you finish, but Beyoncé had one of the best videos of all time!

Knock, knock.

Who's there?

Lionel.

Lionel who?

**Lionel through the keyhole and saw you picking your nose!
Knock, knock.**

Who's there?

Abby.

Abby who?

**Abby birthday to you!
Knock, knock.**

Who's there?

Lego

Lego who?

Lego my eggo!

Knock, knock.

Who's there?

Cantaloupe.

Cantaloupe who?

**Cantaloupe without my permission!
Knock, knock.**

Who's there?

Pudding.

Pudding who?

**Pudding this world behind us!
Knock! Knock!**

Who's There?

Wendy!

Wendy who?

Wendy wind blows the cradle will fall.

Knock! Knock!

Who's There?

Daisy!

Daisy who?

Daisy me rollin, they hatin, tryin to keep me live

KNOCK! KNOCK!

Who's There?

Hello!

Hello who?

Hello from the other side I must've called a thousand times.

Knock! Knock!

Who's There?

Usher!

Usher who?

Usher wish you would let me in.

KNOCK! KNOCK!

Who's There?

Joana!

Joana who?

I Joana close my eyes, I Joana fall asleep 'cause I miss you Babe and I don't wanna miss a thing.

Knock! Knock!

Who's There?

Everybody

Everybody who?

**Everybody was Kung fu fighting!
Knock! Knock!**

Who's There?

Tissue.

Tissue Who?

**All I Want For Christmas Tissue.
Knock! Knock!**

Who's There?

Kenya!

Kenya who?

Kenya feel the love tonight!

Knock! Knock!

Who's There?

Shelby!

Shelby who?

Shelby comin' round the mountain when she comes.

KNOCK! KNOCK!

Who's There?

Barbara!

Barbara who?

**Barbara black sheep have you any wool?
Knock! Knock!**

Who's There?

Ella.

Ella who?

Ella 'bout that bass, 'bout that bass, no treble...

Knock! Knock!

Who's There?

Haze!

Haze who?

For haze a jolly good fellow!
Knock! Knock!

Who's There?

Dishwash.

Dishwash who?

Dishwash for you and me, living out our dream, we're all right where we should be!
Knock! Knock!

Who's There?

Broccoli?

Broccoli who?

Broccoli doesn't have a last name, silly.

Knock! Knock!

Who's There?

Mikey.

Mikey who?

**Mikey doesn't fit in the keyhole!
Knock! Knock!**

Who's there?

Oink oink.

Oink oink who?

**Make up your mind—are you a pig, or an owl?!
Knock! Knock!**

Who's there?

The interrupting cow.

The interrupting cow–

**Moo

Knock! Knock!

Who's There?

Ice cream.

Ice cream who?

**ICE CREAM SO YOU CAN HEAR ME!
Knock! Knock!**

Who's There?

Justin.

Justin who?

**Justin the neighborhood and thought I'd come over!
Knock! Knock!**

Who's there?

Control freak.

Co...

You should say "Control freak who" now

Knock! Knock!

Who's there?

Robin.

Robin who?

**Robin you—hand over the cash!
Knock! Knock!**

Who's There?

Juno.

Juno who?

**Juno how funny this is?
Knock! Knock!**

Who's There?

Watts.

Watts who?

Watts for dinner? I'm hungry.

Knock! Knock!

Who's There?

Whoo.

Whoo-hoo.

**Thank you! Can I get some applause?
Knock! Knock!**

Who's There?

Kanga.

Kanga who?

**I believe it is pronounced kanga-roo.
Knock! Knock!**

Who's There?

Chickens.

Chickens who?

Wrong, silly. Owls hoo. Chickens cluck.

Knock! Knock!

Who's There?

Ruff ruff.

Ruff ruff who?

**Who let the dogs out? I heard barking!
Knock! Knock!**

Who's There?

Ray D.

Ray D. who?

**Ray D or not, here I come.
Knock! Knock!**

Who's There?

Annie.

Annie who?

Annie more jokes? I'm running low here.

Knock! Knock!

Who's there?

Banana.

Banana who?

Knock! Knock!

Who's there?

Banana.

Banana who?

Knock! Knock!

Who's there?

Orange.

Orange who?

Orange you glad I didn't say Banana!

Knock! Knock!

Who's There?

Twit.

Twit who?

**Did anyone else hear an owl?
Knock! Knock!**

Who's There?

Leon.

Leon who?

**Leon me when you're not strong!
Knock! Knock!**

Who's There?

Annie.

Annie who?

Annie thing you can do I can better!

Knock! Knock!

Who's There?

Alex.

Alex who?

**Alex-plain when you open the door!
Knock! Knock!**

Who's There?

Theodore.

Theodore who?

**Theodore wasn't opened so I knocked.
Knock! Knock!**

Who's There?

Olive.

Olive who?

Olive you. Do you love me too?

Knock! Knock!

Who's There?

Matt.

Matt who?

That's my full name, but my friends call me Matt. Knock! Knock!

Who's There?

Iona.

Iona who?

Iona new car! Knock! Knock!

Who's There?

June.

June who?

June know how long I've been knocking out here?

Knock! Knock!

Who's There?

Ben.

Ben who?

**Ben hoping I can come in!
Knock! Knock!**

Who's There?

Aaron.

Aaron who?

Why Aaron you opening the door? Knock! Knock!

Who's There?

Mary.

Mary who?

Mary Christmas!

Knock! Knock!

Who's There?

Abby.

Abby who?

**Abby birthday to you!
Knock! Knock!**

Who's There?

Ferdie!

Ferdie who?

**Ferdie last time open this door.
Knock! Knock!**

Who's There?

Iva.

Iva who?

I've a sore hand from knocking!

Knock! Knock!

Who's There?

Gladys.

Gladys who?

**Gladys Friday, finally the weekend starts!
Knock! Knock!**

Who's There?

Britney Spears.

Britney Spears who?

**Knock, knock – oops I did it again.
Knock! Knock!**

Who's There?

Sadie.

Sadie who?

Sadie magic word and I'll come in!

Knock! Knock!

Who's There?

A little old lady

A little old lady who?

**Wow, I didn't know you could yodel!
Knock! Knock!**

Who's There?

Hawaii

Hawaii who?

**I'm fine, Hawaii you?
Knock! Knock!**

Who's There?

Adore.

Adore who?

Adore is between you and me so please open up!

Knock! Knock!

Who's There?

Hatch.

Hatch who?

God bless you!
Knock! Knock!

Who's There?

Kenya.

Kenya who?

Kenya feel the love tonight?
Knock! Knock!

Who's There?

Icing.

Icing who?

Icing so loudly so everyone can hear me!

Knock! Knock!

Who's There?

Canoe.

Canoe who?

**Canoe come and play? I'm bored!
Knock! Knock!**

Who's There?

A broken pencil.

A broken pencil who?

**Never mind it's pointless.
Knock! Knock!**

Who's There?

Opportunity.

Opportunity doesn't knock twice!

Knock, knock.

Who's there?

Cash.

Cash who?

**No thanks, I prefer peanuts.
Knock, knock.**

Who's there?

Spell.

Spell who?

**W. H. O.
Knock, knock.**

Who's there?

Double.

Double who?

W!

Knock, knock.

Who's there?

Lettuce.

Lettuce who?

**Lettuce in, it's cold out here!
Knock, knock.**

Who's there?

Cow says.

Cow says who?

**No, a cow says mooooo!
Knock, knock.**

Who's there?

To.

To who?

No, it's to whom!

Knock, knock.

Who's there?

Tank.

Tank who?

**You're welcome.
Knock, knock.**

Who's there?

Adore.

Adore who?

**Adore is between you and me, so please open up!
Knock, knock.**

Who's there?

Figs.

Figs who?

Figs the doorbell. I've been knocking forever!

Knock, knock.

Who's there?

Interrupting sloth.

Interrupting sloth who?

(20 seconds of silence)

Slooooooooth.

Knock, knock.

Who's there?

Interrupting pirate.

Interrupting pira-

**ARGHHHHHHHH
Knock, knock.**

Who's there?

Stopwatch.

Stopwatch who?

Stopwatch you're doing and let me in!

Knock, knock.

Who's there?

Says.

Says who?

Says me!
Knock, knock.

Who's there?

Dishes.

Dishes who?

Dishes the police, open up!
Knock, knock.

Who's there?

Woo.

Woo who?

Glad you're excited too!

Knock, knock.

Who's there?

Tennis.

Tennis who?

**Tennis five plus five.
Knock, knock.**

Who's there?

Watts.

Watts who?

**Watts for dinner? I'm hungry.
Knock, knock.**

Who's there?

Who.

Who who?

I didn't know you were an owl!

Knock, knock.

Who's there?

Ketchup.

Ketchup who?

**Ketchup with me and I'll tell you!
Knock, knock.**

Who's there?

Dozen.

Dozen who?

**Dozen anybody want to let me in?
Knock, knock.**

Who's there?

Lena.

Lena who?

Lena a little closer, and I'll tell you another joke!

Knock, knock.

Who's there?

Needle.

Needle who?

Needle little help opening the door! Knock, knock.

Who's there?

Goat.

Goat who?

**Goat to the door and find out!
Knock, knock.**

Who's there?

Beets.

Beets who?

Beets me!

Knock, knock.

Who's there?

You.

You who?

Yoo-hoo! Anybody home?
Knock, knock.

Who's there?

Weekend.

Weekend who?

Weekend do anything we want!
Knock, knock

Who's there?

Butter.

Butter who?

Butter let me in or I'll freeze!

Knock, knock.

Who's there?

Roach.

Roach who?

**Roach you a letter, and I'm putting it in your mailbox!
Knock, knock.**

Who's there?

Abby.

Abby who?

**Abby birthday to you!
Knock, knock.**

Who's there?

Leash.

Leash who?

Leash you could do is answer the doorbell!

Knock, knock.

Who's there?

Radio.

Radio who?

**Radio not, here I come!
Knock, knock.**

Who's there?

Zoom.

Zoom who?

**Zoom did you think it was?
Knock, knock.**

Who's there?

Witches.

Witches who?

Witches the best way out of this neighborhood!?

Knock, knock.

Who's there?

Adam.

Adam who?

Adam my way, I'm coming in! Knock, knock.

Who's there?

Venice.

Venice who?

**Venice your dad coming home?
Knock, knock.**

Who's there?

Sue.

Sue who?

Sue-prize! Happy birthday!

Knock, knock.

Who's there?

Wendy.

Wendy who?

Wendy bell gonna start working again?
Knock, knock.

Who's there?

Bless.

Bless who?

But I didn't sneeze!
Knock, knock

Who's there?

Noah.

Noah who?

Know a place I can spend the night?

Knock, knock.

Who's there?

Water.

Water who?

**Water you asking so many questions for, just open up!
Knock, knock.**

Who's there?

Shore.

Shore who?

**Shore hope you like bad jokes!
Knock, knock.**

Who's there?

Candice.

Candice who?

Candice joke get any worse?

Knock, knock.

Who's there?

Theodore.

Theodore who?

**Theodore wasn't opened so I knocked.
Knock, knock.**

Who's there?

An interrupting cow

An interrupt—

**MOO!
Knock, knock.**

Who's there?

Orange.

Orange who?

Orange you going to let me in?

Knock, knock.

Who's there?

Nobel.

Nobel who?

**Nobel ... that's why I knocked!
Knock, knock.**

Who's there?

Weirdo.

Weirdo who?

**Weirdo you think you're going?
Knock, knock.**

Who's there?

Anita.

Anita who?

Anita use the bathroom, please open the door!

Knock, knock.

Who's there?

Canoe.

Canoe who?

Canoe come out now?
Knock, knock.

Who's there?

Dozen.

Dozen who?

Dozen anyone want to let me in?
Knock, knock.

Who's there?

Alec.

Alec who?

Alectricity. BUZZ!

Knock, knock.

Who's there?

Olive.

Olive who?

**Olive you sooooo much!
Knock, knock.**

Who's there?

Honeydew.

Honeydew who?

**Honeydew you wanna dance?
Knock, knock.**

Who's there?

Ears.

Ears who?

'Ears another knock-knock joke for ya!

Knock, knock.

Who's there?

Cook.

Cook who?

**Yeah, you do sound cuckoo!
Knock, knock.**

Who's there?

Luke.

Luke who?

**Luke through the peephole and find out.
Knock! Knock!**

Who's There?

Pecan

Pecan who?

Pecan someone your own size.

Knock, knock.

Who's there?

Howl.

Howl who?

**Howl you know unless you open the door?
Knock, knock.**

Who's there?

Mikey.

Mikey who?

**Mikey doesn't work, can you let me in?
Knock, knock.**

Who's there?

Ya.

Ya who?

Yippee!

Knock, knock.

Who's there?

Honey bee.

Honey bee who?

**Honey bee a dear and get the door for me.
Knock, knock.**

Who's there?

Icy.

Icy who?

**Icy you in there!
Knock, knock.**

Who's there?

A herd.

A herd who?

A herd you were home, so I came over!

Knock, knock.

Who's there?

Alex.

Alex who?

**Alex-plain later, just open up!
Knock, knock.**

Who's there?

CD.

CD who?

**CD person knocking on the door?
Knock, knock.**

Who's there?

Isabel.

Isabel who?

Isabel not working?

Knock, knock

Who's there?

Ben.

Ben who?

Ben knocking for 10 minutes!
Knock, knock.

Who's there?

Scold.

Scold who?

Scold outside, let me in!
Knock, knock.

Who's there?

Cargo.

Cargo who?

Car go "Toot toot, vroom, vroom!"

Knock, knock.

Who's there?

Nana.

Nana who?

**Nana your business!
Knock, knock.**

Who's there?

A little old lady.

A little old lady who?

**Hey, I didn't know you could yodel!
Knock, knock.**

Who's there?

Hatch.

Hatch who?

Bless you!

Knock, knock.

Who's there?

Alice.

Alice who?

**Alice fair in love and war.
Knock, knock.**

Who's there?

Snow.

Snow who?

**Snow use. The joke is over.
Knock, knock.**

Who's there?

Euripides.

Euripides who?

Euripides clothes, you pay for them!

Knock, knock.

Who's there?

Amos.

Amos who?

**A mosquito. Look, right there!
Knock, knock.**

Who's there?

Dwayne.

Dwayne who?

**Dwayne the sink. I need to use it!
Knock, knock.**

Who's there?

Razor.

Razor who?

Razor hands, this is a stickup!

Knock, knock.

Who's there?

Thermos.

Thermos who?

**Thermos be a better way to get to you.
Knock, knock.**

Who's there?

Amarillo.

Amarillo who?

**Amarillo nice person.
Knock, knock.**

Who's there?

Voodoo.

Voodoo who?

Voodoo you think you are?

Knock, knock.

Who's there?

Cher.

Cher who?

**Cher would be nice if you opened the door!
Knock, knock.**

Who's there?

Mustache.

Mustache who?

**I mustache you a question.
Knock, knock.**

Who's there?

Banana.

Banana who?

Banana split!

Knock, knock.

Who's there?

Beef.

Beef who?

**Before I get cold, you'd better let me in!
Knock, knock.**

Who's there?

Beets!

Beets who?

**Beets me!
Knock, knock.**

Who's there?

Butter.

Butter who?

Butter be quick. I have to go to the bathroom!

Knock, knock.

Who's there?

Cheese.

Cheese who?

**Cheese a nice girl.
Knock, knock.**

Who's there?

Donut.

Donut who?

**Donut ask, it's a secret!
Knock, knock.**

Who's there?

Kiwi.

Kiwi who?

Kiwi go to the store?

Knock, knock.

Who's there?

Olive.

Olive who?

**Olive right next door to you.
Knock, knock.**

Who's there?

Turnip.

Turnip who?

**Turnip the volume, it's quiet in here.
Knock, knock.**

Who's there?

Abe.

Abe who?

Abe C D E F G H...

Knock, knock.

Who's there?

Ada.

Ada who?

**Ada burger for lunch!
Knock, knock.**

Who's there?

Al.

Al who?

**Al give you a high five if you open this door!
Knock, knock.**

Who's there?

Alfie.

Alfie who?

Alfie terrible if you leave!

Knock, knock.

Who's there?

Alma.

Alma who?

Alma not going to say.
Knock, knock.

Who's there?

Amanda.

Amanda who?

A man da fix your doorbell!
Knock, knock.

Who's there?

Barbie.

Barbie Who?

Barbie Q Chicken!

Knock, knock.

Who's there?

Doris.

Doris who?

**Doris locked. Open up, please!
Knock, knock.**

Who's there?

Frank.

Frank who?

**Frank you for being my friend.
Knock, knock.**

Who's there?

Howard.

Howard who?

Howard I know?

Knock, knock.

Who's there?

Joe.

Joe who?

**Joking around with you is one of my favorite things to do!
Knock, knock.**

Who's there?

Otto.

Otto who?

**Otto know what's taking you so long!
Knock, knock.**

Who's there?

Troy.

Troy who?

Troy ringing the doorbell!

Knock, knock.

Who's there?

Tyrone.

Tyrone who?

**Tyrone shoelaces!
Knock, knock.**

Who's there?

Claire.

Claire who?

**Claire the way; I'm coming in!
Knock knock.**

Who's there?

Yah.

Yah who?

No Thanks, I use Google.

Thank You

Thank you for reading 'Knock Knock Jokes for Kids: 200+ FUNNIEST Knock Knock Jokes for Kids.' We hope this book has brought you and your family hours of laughter and joy.

Remember, there's always room for a good joke, so keep these in your back pocket for the next family gathering or road trip.

Don't forget to share the fun with your friends and loved ones, and keep the laughter going! Thank you again for choosing our book, and we hope to see you again soon."

Don't miss out!

Visit the website below and you can sign up to receive emails whenever Issam Ramzi publishes a new book. There's no charge and no obligation.

https://books2read.com/r/B-A-HPWX-MGYHC

BOOKS 2 READ

Connecting independent readers to independent writers.

www.ingramcontent.com/pod-product-compliance
Lightning Source LLC
Chambersburg PA
CBHW052220150726
48002CB00003B/1209